REMEMBERING
SEVEN PROPHETS

Thomas S. Monson

REMEMBERING SEVEN PROPHETS

Thomas S. Monson

MEMORIES OF FRANCIS M. GIBBONS
AS TOLD TO DANIEL BAY GIBBONS

Sixteen Stones Press

HOLLADAY, UTAH

Book layout, typography, and cover design ©2015 by Julie G. Gibbons. Photo credits: all cover photographs from the private collection of Francis M. Gibbons, used by permission. Sixteen Stones Press logo design by Marina Telezar.

Sixteen Stones Press
Publisher website: www.sixteenstonespress.com

Thomas S. Monson
(Remembering Seven Prophets, Book 7)
by Daniel Bay Gibbons

Paperback ISBN 978-1-942640-11-0
eBook ISBN 978-1-942640-12-7

TABLE OF CONTENTS

REMEMBERING SEVEN PROPHETS

This collection of reminiscences about the life of President Thomas Spencer Monson, the sixteenth President of The Church of Jesus Christ of Latter-day Saints is part of a larger work entitled *Remembering Seven Prophets*. This work is the fruit of more than eighty hours of interviews I conducted with my father, Francis M. Gibbons, between the years 2001 to 2011, and then another dozen hours of interviews conducted between July and December of 2014 following my return from presiding over the Russia Novosibirsk Mission of the Church.

"A Plutarch to the Presidents of the Church"

Now in his ninety-fifth year, Francis M. Gibbons is perhaps the greatest student on the lives of the Presidents of the Church in this dispensation. He has two unique qualifications to speak and write about the Prophets.

First, over the past forty-five years, my father has become "a Plutarch to the Presidents of the Church." This unusual phrase has reference to Plutarch, the ancient Greek writer, who became the most famous biographer in history, the "Father of Biography." Many years ago my father shared with my mother his special aspiration to become "a Plutarch to the Presidents of the Church, and through their lives to write the history of the Church." If any man or woman deserves the title "Plutarch to the Presidents of the Church," it is my father, Francis M. Gibbons. Over the past four decades he has become by far the most prolific writer of biographies of the Presidents of the Church, writing a full-length biography of every Prophet from Joseph Smith to Gordon B. Hinckley. Dad's biographies of the Prophets have been very popular, selling many hundreds of thousands of copies. Thirteen of his presidential biographies have been included in Brigham Young University's list of "Sixty Significant Mormon Biographies." He has truly become "a Plutarch to the Presidents of the Church."

"A Scribe to the Prophets"

Second, my father has been a personal witness and observer of the character of the last seven Presidents of the Church:

Presidents Joseph Fielding Smith, Harold B. Lee, Spencer W. Kimball, Ezra Taft Benson, Howard W. Hunter, Gordon B. Hinckley, and Thomas S. Monson. He knew these men personally. He worked with them. While serving from 1970 to 1986 as the secretary to the First Presidency and later as a member of the Seventy, Dad associated with them on a daily basis. He was a "Scribe to the Prophets," as were William Clayton, Wilford Woodruff, Joseph F. Smith, William F. Gibbons, Joseph Anderson, and others before him.

"I am their witness"

When Dad was sustained as a General Authority in April of 1986, after many years serving as the faithful scribe for the Presidents of the Church, he said:

> The Church is led by prophets, seers, and revelators. I am their witness. I testify that they are honorable, upright, dedicated men of integrity committed to teaching the principles of the gospel, who strive with all of their might to prepare a people ready for the return of the head of the Church, Jesus Christ, at His second coming.

This work, *Remembering Seven Prophets*, shares many unique stories, anecdotes, insights, and testimonies about the last seven Presidents of the Church, which are nowhere else available.

I offer this work for the enlightenment and inspiration of the reader and as a tribute to the memory of the seven Presidents of the Church featured in these pages. I love and honor these great men and add my witness to that of my father that they were and are Prophets of God!

Daniel Bay Gibbons
August 4, 2015
Holladay, Utah

CHRONOLOGY OF THE LIFE OF PRESIDENT THOMAS S. MONSON

August 21, 1927
Thomas Spencer Monson is born in Salt Lake City, Utah, to G. Spencer and Gladys Condie Monson.

March 15, 1944
President Thomas S. Monson receives his patriarchal blessing.

Fall 1944
President Thomas S. Monson enrolls at the University of Utah and meets Frances Beverly Johnson.

1945-1946
President Thomas S. Monson completes his naval training.

1948
President Thomas S. Monson graduates from the University of Utah and begins working at the Deseret News as a classified advertising manager.

October 7, 1944

President Thomas S. Monson marries Frances Beverly Johnson in the Salt Lake Temple.

March 12, 1950

President Thomas S. Monson is sustained as the second counselor to Bishop John R. Burt in the Sixth-Seventh Ward of the Temple View Stake.

May 1950

President Thomas S. Monson is called and ordained as bishop of the Sixth-Seventh Ward at age twenty-two, after serving in the bishopric for only two months. He serves for five years, until **July of 1950**. At the time, President Monson is the youngest bishop in the Church.

June 1955

President Thomas S. Monson is called as second counselor to Percy K. Fetzer in the presidency of the Temple View Stake. He serves until **June of 1957**.

April 1959
President Thomas S. Monson serves as president of the Canadian Mission. He serves until **January of 1962**.

1962
President Thomas S. Monson is named General Manager of the Deseret News Press.

October 4, 1963
President Thomas S. Monson is sustained as a member of the Quorum of the Twelve Apostles. He is ordained on **October 10, 1963**.

1968 to 1985
President Thomas S. Monson supervises the work in Europe.

14 June 1969
President Thomas S. Monson organizes the Dresden Mission with Henry Burkhardt as president.

1976 to 1982
President Thomas S. Monson serves as chairman of the Missionary Committee.

June 29, 1985

President Thomas S. Monson participates in the dedication of the Freiberg Germany Temple.

November 10, 1985

President Thomas S. Monson is sustained and set apart as second counselor to President Ezra Taft Benson.

June 5, 1994

President Thomas S. Monson is sustained and set apart as second counselor to President Howard W. Hunter.

March 12, 1995

President Thomas S. Monson is sustained and set apart as first counselor to President Gordon B. Hinckley.

February 3, 2008

President Thomas S. Monson is ordained and set apart as the sixteenth President of the Church.

"I HAVE A NEW BISHOP FOR *YOU!*"

It is well known that President Thomas S. Monson was called as a bishop in the Church at age twenty-two. What is less well known is that his mother, Gladys Monson, predicted his call on the date of President Monson's birth. As she lay in St. Mark's hospital with her newborn son on a Sunday morning in 1927, her husband, G. Spencer Monson, reported to her that a new bishop had been installed in Church that day. The mother's response was, "I have a new bishop for *you!*"

"A BISHOP LONG ON CARING AND SHORT ON STATISTICS"

President Thomas S. Monson was the youngest bishop in the Church when called as a bishop at age twenty-two. His ward was on the west side of Salt Lake City where there were many unemployed members and eighty-five widows. I understand that President Monson's ward had the largest welfare responsibility in the Church at the time. There, in that humble little ward, President Monson learned the principles of welfare and caring in a very practical way. He was a bishop long on caring and short on statistics.

Bishop Monson laid into his new duties as a bishop with great vigor. He began to visit each member of his flock, one by one, and to instill a sense of love and community in the neighborhood. He gave particular care to the fatherless and the widows in the ward. I believe that his care of his widows stands as the most enduring accomplishment of his service. Each Christmastime, he would call personally at the home of each widow, leaving them a gift and a bishop's blessings. After his release, this practice continued down through the years. I can attest that even when he was a member of the Twelve and in the First Presidency, he continued, year by year, to visit the former members of his flock. He would usually take a week of his vacation in order to visit all of the widows each Christmas season.

"HAVE COURAGE, MY BOY, TO SAY YES"

After serving as a bishop, President Monson was called as a counselor in the stake presidency of the Temple View Stake in June of 1955, when he was twenty-eight years old. The first notice he had of the call was when his name was read from the stand in the Assembly Hall. The presiding authority was President Joseph Fielding Smith, then a member of the Twelve, who announced the new stake president, Percy K. Fetzer. Then, presenting the counselors, President Smith announced Thomas S. Monson as the new second counselor, saying, "Bishop Monson knows nothing of this appointment, but if he will accept it, we will be pleased to hear from him now!" President Monson, caught totally unaware of his new calling, had to improvise. Walking to the pulpit, he paused and then referred to the song which had just been sung in the conference, whose lyrics admonished adherence to the Word of Wisdom: "Have courage, my boy, to say no." This became President Monson's text for his impromptu sermon, which he developed into the theme, "Have courage, my boy, to say yes!"

This early sermon of the Prophet can be seen as a theme for his entire ministry. Have the courage to say yes. It beautifully illustrates the positive, energetic, happy, and courageous aspects of President Monson's personality and service.

"HE CLEARLY SAW TOM MONSON SITTING ON THE END SEAT"

In 1973 I attended the funeral services for Elder Thomas S. Monson's mother, Gladys Monson, which were held in the Rosecrest Ward chapel. While there, I learned these additional inspirational details regarding his 1955 call to the Temple View Stake Presidency.

One of the speakers, Brother John R. Burt, who served in the Temple View Stake presidency with President Monson, told this unusual story about his call: Brother Burt had preceded President Monson as bishop of the Sixth-Seventh Ward, and in fact President Monson had served briefly as Brother Burt's counselor, so the two men were well acquainted. At the reorganization of the stake presidency, President Joseph Fielding Smith, who effected the change, asked the new stake president, Percy K. Fetzer, to nominate counselors. He immediately chose John R. Burt, a former bishop, but was uncertain about the second counselor. Finally, pressed for time, President Fetzer said that the only other man who came to his mind was Bishop

Thomas S. Monson. President Smith then asked Brother Burt if he could work side by side with President Monson. Brother Burt smiled, because he had already served in a bishopric with Thomas S. Monson, and then enthusiastically endorsed President Fetzer's nomination.

Later that day, as Brother Burt looked at a picture of the interior of the Salt Lake Tabernacle, which hung on the wall of the stake center, he said that he clearly saw, as if in vision, the seats where the Twelve Apostles sit, and he testified that he clearly saw Tom Monson sitting on the end seat.

On the morning before Elder Monson was sustained as a member of the Quorum of the Twelve in October of 1963, Brother Burt called his wife, who asked if he knew who the new member of the Twelve would be. Without any prior knowledge other than that received through the Spirit in 1955, he said, "Tom Monson."

"A SPECIAL YOUNG MAN"

Very early in his life, President Thomas S. Monson caught the caught the eye of the leading Brethren of the Church. While he was still in his early thirties, he was called as the president of the mission whose headquarters were in Toronto, Canada. In those days, released mission presidents reported directly to the First Presidency, so President Monson met personally with President David O. McKay and his counselors when he returned home from Toronto.

While I was writing the biography of President McKay, I was given access to all of his private diaries. President McKay made one entry in which he mentioned young Thomas S. Monson, and he made the comment that he was "a special young man," and that the Brethren should "keep their eye on him."

"A GREAT LOVE AND ADMIRATION FOR PRESIDENT CLARK"

Shortly after his mission to Canada, President Monson was called to serve on two of the general Church councils (missionary and home teaching), for which he regularly attended stake conferences with General Authorities, who had the opportunity to watch him in action. At the same time, he was the manager of the Deseret News Press, which brought him in contact with General Authorities whose books were being prepared for publication.

President Monson often spoke of his shepherding one of President J. Reuben Clark's books, *Our Lord of the Gospels*, through the process of publication. From that experience and perhaps others, he acquired a great love and admiration for President Clark. His youngest son is Clark Monson, named after President Clark. So in the months and years after his mission, President Monson's daily work and his weekend work brought him into regular contact with the highest leaders of the Church. Given President Monson's great talents and spirituality and the deep impression he had made on President McKay, it is not surprising that he would be called to the Twelve. But I would go further to say that Thomas S. Monson was one of the great and noble ones selected by God in the preexistence to come to the earth and to lead out in building the Kingdom of God on earth.

"A CONSUMMATE TEAM PLAYER"

President Thomas S. Monson was a reserve basketball player on the University of Utah team that won the 1947 National Invitational Tournament. In those days the NIT was far more prestigious than that of the National Collegiate Athletic Association, or NCAA.

President Monson has always been a consummate team player. He is as enthusiastic sitting on the bench as he is on the court, so to speak. I have often pondered his role as a reserve basketball player and thought it mirrored his history in Church leadership over the course of his ministry. For more than two decades he was a "bench player," so to speak, laboring as a member of the Twelve, following his team leaders. Then, in November of 1985, he was suddenly placed "in the game" as a counselor to President Ezra Taft Benson. It was inspiring to observe him at this juncture in his service. Like a good "reserve player" coming off the bench, he was ready in every way to take a leading role.

"HE WAS CALLED TO THE ATTENTION OF PRESIDENT McKAY"

President Monson once told me that in his opinion he was called to the attention of President McKay by two unusual events: First, he was called upon to report his mission to Canada before the First Presidency almost a year after his release, but just a few months before his call to the Twelve. Second, he said by chance he was able to conduct President McKay on a tour of the new plant at the Deseret News Press, where he worked, not too long before he was called.

"He did say 'Quorum of the Twelve,' didn't he?"

President Monson was called as a member of the Quorum of the Twelve in October of 1963, when he was just 36 years old. President Monson once shared with me this insight about his call:

When President David O. McKay extended the calling, he told Thomas S. Monson that because he, too, had been called to the apostleship as a very young man, he could understand the trauma through which Elder Monson would pass. Afterwards, as President Monson left the Prophet's office, the first person he saw was Henry Smith of the *Deseret News*, who had been confidentially notified of President Monson's call and who was there to get information to fill in the gaps for an article about the new appointment to the Quorum of the Twelve. President Monson told me that when he saw Henry, who was an old friend, he wanted to be sure it was a call to the Twelve and not as an Assistant to the Twelve! President Monson said to Henry, "He did say Quorum of the Twelve, didn't he?"

"I WANTED TO TELL HER ABOUT THE CALLING IN THAT SPECIAL PLACE"

Shortly before his call to the First Presidency, President Monson shared with me this additional detail about his call to the Twelve in 1963. After receiving his call from President David O. McKay, he debated about how to share this earth-shaking news with his wife, Frances Monson. He decided to take her for a drive to the This is the Place Monument at the mouth of Emigration Canyon on the foothills overlooking the Salt Lake Valley. There, they got out of the car and walked around the monument, looking at the statuary and the bronze inscriptions. Finally, after President and Sister Monson had been there for some time in silence, she finally said, "What's wrong?" President Monson then told her about his new calling.

President Monson told me, "I just felt that I wanted to tell her about the calling in that special place."

"SOME FAR-REACHING EVENT WOULD SOON OCCUR IN HIS LIFE"

I once asked President Monson if he had any premonition or hint that he was to be called as a member of the Twelve. He said that he had not, although he had felt rather unsettled for several weeks before the call. He told me that the Sunday before he met with President McKay, he went to his church meetings, as usual, but during the meetings he had the subconscious feeling that he would prefer to be elsewhere, doing something other than church work. It was almost as if he was being tempted away from his path of duty. But praying within himself, the negative feeling passed, and he told me that at that moment, he was filled with a feeling of deep peace and satisfaction that he was in his place doing his duty in the Church, even though he might have preferred to be elsewhere. With these feelings, he said, came an impression that some far-reaching event would soon occur in his life.

"The youngest Apostle for twenty-one years"

After his call to the Quorum of the Twelve in 1963, President Monson brought an unusual youth to the Quorum of the Twelve. Only thirty-six years old at his ordination, he was the youngest Apostle for twenty-one years, from 1963 until the call of Elder Dallin H. Oaks in April of 1984.

When Elder Oaks was called, it was the first time in a generation that a person younger than President Monson sat in the circle. Still, President Monson is only about five years older than Elder Oaks.

"A HAPPY WARRIOR"

President Monson has a very happy, positive, enthusiastic personality. He always radiates an unusual cheerfulness from his countenance. His attitude is always upbeat, always optimistic. In my decades of personal interaction with him, I never once saw him depressed or disappointed. He has the personality of a "happy warrior." No obstacle seems too difficult for him to surmount. He is whole souled, able, sincere, and a great catalyst among the Brethren and all the membership of the Church.

This radiant, cheerful personality in President Monson is contagious. Just being around him causes people to become hopeful and enthusiastic. I suppose this quality in President Monson might be called "charisma," but it is really more than that. He is a truly converted soul, with a love the Lord and His Gospel.

"THOMAS S. MONSON REMINDED ME OF THE PROPHET JOSEPH SMITH"

For sixteen years, while serving as secretary to the First Presidency, I sat on the stand in the Salt Lake Tabernacle facing the speakers' stand from the side. From that vantage point, I saw all of the speakers in profile. Over and over through the years, the features of Thomas S. Monson reminded me of the Prophet Joseph Smith. From the various portraits we have of the Prophet Joseph, and especially from the profile paintings done in Nauvoo, he had a striking profile with a towering physique, a regal bearing, prominent features of nose and chin, and an aura of confidence and cheerfulness. The countenance of President Monson, seen in profile, had the same qualities.

But, the similarities between the Prophet Joseph and President Monson do not end there. His friendliness, interest in people, his common touch, his energy, and compassion are of a kind that matches the qualities of the Prophet Joseph. These qualities naturally attracted followers both to the Prophet Joseph and to President Monson.

"THE CORDIALITY AND FRIENDLINESS OF PRESIDENT MONSON"

I first met President Thomas S. Monson in the Upper Room of the Salt Lake Temple on April 9, 1970, the date I began my service as the secretary to the First Presidency. On that morning, I was taken around the circle by President Harold B. Lee and introduced to each member of the Quorum of the Twelve before the beginning of the Council Meeting. I was impressed by the cordiality and friendliness of President Monson. He was very open and warm. A bond of friendship and mutual admiration grew up between us. I soon developed a very close relationship with him. He often called me or visited me in my office to counsel about the work. As the frequency of these and other contacts increased, the nature of our relationship became one of a more confidential kind. Such was the trust between us that we shared matters of the most sensitive kind pertaining to the work that I never felt free to record nor discuss. I believe that I became his confidant and sounding board on many subjects.

One of the things I enjoyed most about my work with the Brethren was my association with President Monson. From the beginning we had a special understanding and camaraderie. I treasured my relationship with President Monson and never want to betray it. I admire and respect him and fully sustain him in his prophetic office.

"My mentor"

Beginning in the early 1970s, I began, in the early mornings, to write a biography of the Prophet Joseph Smith. I had never written a full-length biography before, and this project was undertaken on my own time to fulfill a long-held ambition to write about the Prophet.

Over time, I shared this private endeavor with President Monson, and he began to play a key role in this aspect of my life. During the years I labored over this project, President Monson would often inquire about it and offer me encouragement. Then, in the mid 1970s when my manuscript was completed, he offered to read it to give me his honest appraisal. Thus began a long literary mentorship with President Monson. He offered several suggestions to me, which I welcomed. This first biography of the Prophet Joseph Smith was ultimately published in 1977, and in the succeeding years I wrote and saw published biographies of fourteen of Joseph Smith's successors.

President Monson became my mentor and kindly offered to review my manuscripts. For my part I gladly accepted because of his experience as the manager of the Deseret News Press, as a member of the board of the Deseret Book Company, and as an aide in shepherding many books through to press for President J. Reuben Clark and others. President Monson reviewed all of my manuscripts about Presidents of the Church up until the time he became a member of the First Presidency in late 1985. He probably would have reviewed the later manuscripts, had I asked him, but I was reluctant to do so, for fear of burdening him or causing him embarrassment.

It will be found that most of my biographies express indebtedness to the "Mentor," who was President Thomas S. Monson. Only my wife, Helen, knew the identity of the "Mentor" for certain. Others may have guessed at it. Only two people had the nerve to ask me who my "Mentor" was, and I declined to reveal to them that it was President Thomas S. Monson.

I am grateful for President Monson's support and for all he has done to help me in my endeavors to write the lives of the Presidents of the Church.

"A VERY SKILLED ADMINISTRATOR"

President Thomas S. Monson is a very skilled administrator. He has always had the ability to inspire confidence, and to create and maintain unity in a group. He also has one of the most positive and enthusiastic personalities I have ever encountered. In all my years of close association with him, I never saw him depressed or disappointed. He is also a man of great integrity. There is no pretense in his makeup. What the membership of the Church sees of him in public is the same in private.

I would say that President Monson has the skill of a good chess player—he is able to envision future moves. He is very adept at long-range planning. And, like a good chess player, he sometimes achieves his goals through indirection or adroit maneuvering. President Monson is a very tough man, a very strong personality. Once he knows what he wants to achieve and how to do it, he is relentless.

"HE RECOGNIZES, ENCOURAGES AND BUILDS UP"

In his relationships with people, President Thomas S. Monson always remembers and lifts.

President Monson has a phenomenal memory for names. I have seen him instantly recall the names of people he met briefly decades before. To hear a Prophet of God recall and speak your name is a powerful motivation. It is one of his natural gifts.

President Monson not only remembers names, he also lifts people up. He is a builder of men and women. He recognizes, encourages, and builds up his followers in very personal ways. I have seen him go out of his way countless times to lift people up and to recognize them. He is especially apt to recognize and uplift those who are laboring in obscure roles. In this respect, President Monson reminds me of the story of the Savior, who saw the man "of little stature" called Zacchaeus, who climbed a sycamore tree by the side of the road in order to catch a glimpse of the Lord over the heads of the taller people who were pressing close to the Lord. The Lord "looked up" and saw the little man in the tree, publicly recognized him, and invited him to dine with him. (See Luke 19:1-10).

I was often the recipient of President Monson's out-of-the-way kindnesses as I worked in a relatively obscure role at Church headquarters. For example, on one rare occasion I was asked to share my testimony in a Council Meeting with the Brethren. Afterwards, President Monson went out of his way to share with me a special poetic couplet he had composed:

Vision without work is daydreaming.
Work without vision is drudgery.
Vision coupled with work brings success.

After sharing this little saying with me, President Monson told me that it exemplified my service to the Brethren. This moved me deeply, and I later had this couplet engraved on special plaques, which I gave to all of my children. This was a great motivation to me. It exemplified one of the most salient leadership qualities of his ministry. How many people would take the time to seek out a relatively obscure person, laboring in the Kingdom, and then pay them a compliment, such as I received from President Monson? I have no doubt that the experience I had with President

Monson has been repeated thousands of times through the years with others in similar contexts. The effect of this action of President Monson is to create a strong bond of love and loyalty and to provide an incentive to do better.

"THEY OFTEN SHOWED DEFERENCE TO YOUNG THOMAS S. MONSON"

This feeling that President Monson was "a special young man" was shared by many of the Brethren during the early years of his service in the Quorum of the Twelve. I noted that the senior members of the First Presidency and the Twelve often showed deference to young Thomas S. Monson, although he was still in his thirties and forties. The respect they gave him belied his relatively junior status.

An example of this deference could be detected in President N. Eldon Tanner. Though he had served as a counselor to four Presidents of the Church and was a man of honorable age and significant accomplishment and ability, I noted that President Tanner never criticized President Monson in my presence. This was unusual for President Tanner, as he was a very straight-shooting, frank, and outspoken man, and his leadership style was to freely correct those with whom he worked, including members of the Twelve. But not so with President Monson—President

Tanner treated him with the highest respect and deference. This was also true with President Marion G. Romney, who always spoke with equal praise about President Monson.

"THE MOST AGGRESSIVE MEMBER OF THE TWELVE"

After beginning my service with the Brethren in April of 1970, I soon learned that the most assertive member of the Quorum was Thomas S. Monson. Over time I became more and more impressed with his great leadership abilities. He was very aggressive and a driver, but he also had the great ability to draw people together and to make them feel a part of what was going on. Sometimes his aggressiveness and energy had the effect of exhausting those who worked with him, but he seemed to be sensitive of this feeling; and when he became aware of even a hint of a negative reaction setting in, he withdrew and then went out of his way to bridge any gap that may have opened up. In this way, he never made any enemies, but only friends and supporters.

"A SWEEPING CHANGE IN THE WAY THE CHURCH OPERATED"

In the early 1980s, when President Gordon B. Hinckley was the only physically active member of the First Presidency, President Monson stepped up to take a strong leadership role in the Quorum of the Twelve. This was a period of significant challenge and opportunity in the Church, brought about in large part by the unprecedented growth in the membership of the Church, which had begun in the administration of President David O. McKay and greatly accelerated during the administrations of Presidents Joseph Fielding Smith, Harold B. Lee, and especially Spencer W. Kimball. The explosive growth of the Church was straining the then-existing administrative structure of the Church at the headquarters level, and it was also spreading thin the time and energy of the General Authorities.

In about 1983, President Monson chaired a committee that prepared a very significant report for the First Presidency. This report proposed significant administrative changes in the work. These changes included the establishment of Area Presidencies in the international areas of the Church and the elimination of artificial distinctions between ecclesiastical and temporal affairs. These proposals from President Monson's committee, which were ultimately implemented in substance, brought about a sweeping change in the way the Church operated at the highest level.

"THE GIFT OF MAKING THE GOSPEL CLEAR TO THE MASSES"

President Thomas S. Monson is extremely articulate and expresses himself freely and convincingly. His General Conference talks are masterpieces of clarity and inspiration. They strike a near perfect tone between the colloquial and the sublime. In many ways, his sermons are reminiscent of the powerful sermons of the greatest orators of Church history, in days before microphones or recording devices.

President Monson once shared with me that his patriarchal blessing promised that he would have a special gift of "making the gospel clear to the masses." In fulfillment of this patriarchal promise, President Monson does have a very clear, simple means of exposition, which could hardly be misunderstood. His talks are also delivered with great enthusiasm and fervor and are never read. He may memorize them, or at least have them so well in mind that he delivers them flawlessly without benefit of notes.

"PRESIDENT MONSON LITERALLY PRAYED DURING THE ENTIRE JOURNEY"

During his years in the Twelve, President Thomas S. Monson was one of the most physically active and widely traveled of all members of the Twelve, with special assignments in Europe. In this assignment he often traveled to Europe to create stakes or dedicate new areas for the preaching of the gospel. For example, he once traveled to Portugal to offer a dedicatory prayer in that land. But there was no nation closer to his heart than East Germany, where he had a multitude of special spiritual experiences.

Elder Joseph B. Wirthlin, who as an Assistant to the Twelve assisted President Monson in the work in East Germany, told me about this special experience he had with the future Prophet in 1978: At that time it was very difficult for the Church to arrange for President Monson and Elder Wirthlin to travel to the Communist-held East Germany, and after one trip it appeared it might not be legally possible for the Brethren to return. However, during their trip, Brother Walter

Krause, the sole Patriarch in East Germany, came to President Monson and Elder Wirthlin before they left and promised them in the name of the Lord that they would both be back together in East Germany.

Elder Wirthlin told me that he had the same impression, that the way would be opened for them both to go back. He also told me that President Monson literally prayed during the entire journey that they would be permitted to return. This prayer, and the prophecies of Brother Krause and Elder Wirthlin were fulfilled within a few months.

"President Monson's advocacy for a future temple in East Germany"

Through more than a decade, President Monson became a strong advocate for the humble saints of East Germany in the leading councils of the Church. This is nowhere more evident than in President Monson's advocacy for a future temple in East Germany.

The saints in East Germany at the time were under the leadership of Henry Burkhardt, the longtime president of the East German Mission. During one of President Monson's trips there, President Burkhardt expressed the strong desire that the worthy members in that country be permitted to receive their endowments and sealings, even though they did not have access to a Temple. At the time it was virtually impossible for citizens of East Germany to obtain exit visas to leave the country for any reason. I was present on several occasions when President Monson spoke privately with President Kimball about the desires of the faithful East German saints.

After his discussion with President Monson, President Kimball really took hold of the idea of helping the East German saints receive temple ordinances. The Prophet gave a great deal of thought to how the Brethren might administer the ordinances and blessings of the endowment and marriage sealings upon worthy members behind the Iron Curtain, despite the lack of a temple there.

Within a year President Monson was able to put into President Burkhardt's hands architectural plans for a small temple to be submitted to the East German officials. This resulted in the miraculous construction and dedication of the Freiberg Temple in 1985.

None of this would have occurred but for the passionate advocacy of President Thomas S. Monson.

"PRESIDENT MONSON TOLD ME THAT HE HAD A VIVID DREAM"

For many years President Monson had a special role as a member of the Quorum of the Twelve with responsibility for the welfare program of the Church. In this role, he worked very closely with President J. Reuben Clark and President Harold B. Lee, two of the earliest visionaries and architects of the program. My sense is that both President Clark and President Lee saw President Monson as the next generation of leadership in welfare matters. Because of this, both of these senior Brethren took President Monson under their wings, and he received special tutelage from both of them. They also expected a great deal from President Monson and even pushed him in sometimes-uncomfortable ways, but he responded with great obedience and humility and quickly developed great leadership skills.

Several years after the death of President Harold B. Lee, President Monson told me that he had a vivid dream, to which he attached great spiritual significance. He said that in his dream, President Harold B. Lee appeared to him. President Lee did not speak, but merely smiled benignly at President Monson, in a way that imparted to him that he was pleased with the way in which the welfare program was developing. President Monson was very moved when he related the circumstances of this dream.

ABOUT THE AUTHOR

Daniel Bay Gibbons is a writer living in Holladay, Utah. The youngest son of Francis M. Gibbons and Helen Bay Gibbons, he is a former trial attorney and judge and is the author of several previous books. He has served as a full-time missionary, twice as a bishop, and as president of the Russia Novosibirsk Mission.

INDEX

Printed in Great Britain
by Amazon